C O

A SLOW GREEN SLEEP

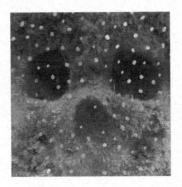

JONATHAN WEINERT

Distributed by Independent Publishers Group
Chicago

Saturnalia Books
105 Woodside Rd.
Ardmore, PA 19003
info@saturnaliabooks.com

ISBN: 978-1-947817-26-5 (print) 978-1-947817-27-2 (ebook)
Library of Congress Control Number: 2020949448

Cover art and book design by Robin Vuchnich

Distributed by:
Independent Publishing Group
814 N. Franklin St.
Chicago, IL 60610
800-888-4741

If I were not human I would not be ashamed of anything

—*W. S. Merwin*

GREEN SWOON

When we were dead, our vexed
tongues hung limp.
You'd made your done face, more or less,
and that was it.

We slept a slow green sleep.
And then the grass grew bronze and stiff
and all we knew was grass
and the ways through grass
and the small strange laws of sleep.

There the ferns grew like hair on the heads of the old dead.
The young dead ate their jam of fig and white cheese.
We wrote our odes and told our jokes
and laughed or rolled our hard white eyes.

You'd think we'd grow as tired of this as we had in life.
But when the weird bell called
and the halls of the dead were filled with the smells
of pine and moss, then how
we loved our deaths the more
and kept on in the ways of death
and left the chance of new life to the ones
who weren't yet done with time.

We were. We'd get in bed there,
in the grass town of the dead,
left leg to right leg, sex to sex,
and let death flow from chest to chest,
a cold sweet air we had no need to breathe,
and hold it there in a deep green swoon
while the earth filled up with dust
and passed through an age of dust
on its way to the last days of dust.

2012

One hundred fifteen in the shade, all day. Burn holes
lace the rose leaves; tomatoes blacken on their stakes.
The citizens of Denver, Phoenix, Santa Fe,
pent inside their malls like spiders under glass,
refuse to read the mortal edicts of the heat.

The landscape bides its own destruction. In a pit,
some thousand bones of hominins and wildebeests
lie twinned together, casual and intimate,
beside the faintest tracing of a dried-up pool.
The same old news: the earth could shrug us lightly off.

Two thousand acres burn toward Colorado Springs.
We humans love the wrongest things: eternity,
our histories, our brains. Indifferent tides will crush
the cordillera in a million years, before
the whole thing ices up, erasing us. Love *that*.

TILTED CITY

The things we passed by every day
outlasted us: comb-teeth scattered
in the gravel, bits of plastic from a laptop.

When our walls came down our shadows
vanished: centuries of slow corrosion,
not the action of our hit-to-kill

materiel. Before our windows all went black
we grew so tired; we wanted clouds for beds
and hills for pillows, valleys

where the very wolves would warm us
and adore us.

———————————

We walked our sons to parks down quiet lanes
and held them when their fear and shame
seemed everything.

We watched their unoffending legs
go flashing down the playgrounds
—boys: those keepers of the cold

white flowers, deep rememberers,
who stepped on grass and laughed,
their girl-limbs bright and pliable

as they climbed the blood-red rungs
and shuddered at the heights.

_____

We wanted beauty in ourselves,
and slow green sleep. Some wanted blood.
We wanted beauty in ourselves

and others' blood. We wanted rest,
and others' grief. We wanted terror
elsewhere, peace at home, the ceaseless

hiss of rain on leaves. The sky kept
going overhead, a lesson in allegiance
we never learned. The roadbeds trembled

on the earth's hot core, our shadows
lay down in the streets and slept.

_____

We sent our circuitry over all the earth.
We sent our weapons, our machines.
Inside, we still were wet and animal;

inside, our boys were wet and animal,
and they climbed on metal bars
and shouted at the darkness. Every face

a cold white flower, hands electric
with the fervor of their play,
great creators of the moment,

establishers of paradise, fallers-down-on-grass,
fierce criers, pedallers, untried cadets.

———————————

We sent our certainty over all the earth.
We sent our idols, our latrines.
Inside, we still were dark and liminal;

inside, our boys were dark and liminal,
and they dreamed on blocks of foam
of seas they'd never seen,

of beaked and big-eyed swimmers,
and they'd wake up finned and razor-toothed,
they worshipped at the Church of Red

Imaginary Creatures, stingray boys in PJs
biding time until the sirens called their names.

———————

Now the sifters' nervous fingers find our stuff:
ballpoint pen caps, cellphone chipsets,
diapers, filings, clickers, toilet seats,

the petrified remains of hot-drink cups
and plastic bags, palimpsests of ads
and patents, hood medallions, dipsticks,

gaskets, nylons, Scrabble pieces, septic tanks,
Kindle cases, keypads, mounded bones of dogs
and cats, cables, jackets, piping, Tyvek,

copper flashing, slabs with writings on them,
diamonds, poisons, gold from domes . . .

———————

We slept while fifteen hundred years
passed over us. No one living
knows our names, or what we saw,

or how it was with us. The sifters,
bending to their cuts and fills,
expose and comb and analyze,

but cannot speak to us.
So much obliterated love,
the scraped uncertain contexts,

the cold white flowers of our ankle bones
emerging from the dirt.

THE STORY OF MY LIFE

It has to do with the shape of a cloud
and the color of rain light
and the fog running its long tongue over the grass

To go fully into the cloud
To go fully into the rain
To go fully into the grass

Mom
I'm going
Dad

———————————

I held my teddy bear in one cold hand

A delicate translucent bubble swirled with primrose and crimson
drifted over the grass
I watched it stretch and thin and rupture
surrendering its crumb of soap

———————————

A shadow came straight out of a pine tree
as bright as daylight in the daylight world

Shadow firehounds moved in the shadow
and accepted my presence as a feature of the presence

I loved their indifference
how they didn't look up from sniffing the blinding grass

how they didn't hurry or scare as I always scared

———————————

Human bone makes a net of shadow
and the brain nests its meager light atop it

which is the way I saw it
from the limb of a pine

———————————

A lake that once showed the face of a meadow
A meadow that once showed the face of a lake

Dead pines driven through the mat like splinters of whitegray bone

I could see where the shoreline once inscribed its sentence along a bank
all crazed and dried up now

A kingdom for milkweed and lichen and spider and mold

The wind rolled down from an invisible peak
and shook yellow powders from the ragwort and ivory fibers from the milkweed

I could see the dark inherent in the noon
the implied twilight

————————————

Some clock other than the kitchen clock
advanced its hands of bone
and in that time
I could see the shadow
that never left the surface of the world

Who could I tell
My eyes grew huge with seeing
and my mouth held words
that nobody could understand

————————————

In the library always a book would say
something like what I couldn't
but then it would veer away
into character and plot

I wanted to stay with the dawn light rising over Indiana hills
and the horizons of rounded shadows sweeping the valleys
when the boy and his sister entered the rocket ship
standing out in an abandoned airfield

not the launch or whatever came after
which I now forget
but the color of the light and the long shadows
and the quiet that surrounded the ship

LINED UP JUST SO

If in the next world we will refuse to matter,
we matter to ourselves in this one,
like several species of migratory birds

sharing the same hierarchy of wires
with evening falling if not exactly sooner
then with greater delicacy

on the last oaks' proffered limbs,
as we prefer. However soon
the memories of cities leave us

isn't soon enough. Nomadic without religion,
mosaic in all accepted senses of the word,

we share the darkness
with a dozen unreal terrors that are worse.
So much that's beautiful has been lost,

but then there are these shadows in the grass
mimicking triumphal marbles that have fallen,
rising to the level of beauty by virtue

only of their absence. Beauty's now
an eye-high sort of style, a peering
through an afterimage, lensless,

or it's notarized and standard, a contract
nobody intends to honor, not these several

kinds of songbirds cracking seeds of darkness
in their beaks. Tending to the humors
of our less immediate natures

blunts the passage of a recollected impulse
to make too much sense of sensation
while the swallows, swifts, and winged victories

inhabit an imperceptible air
like certain wall-drawings downtown
that no one can interpret.

Recognition places us in fields
of various colorings, characters

in separate plays where words no longer turn
to bits and pentacles.
So much that's beautiful has been lost,

as color's lost to the blind from birth,
an absence unfelt and so impossible to name.
Monadic without unity, fractured

in all accepted senses of the world,
we mass together, taken in the aggregate
like corn or bullets,

as though the storehouse of another's face
contained commodities one needs.

If in the next world stones are lives
then dead things still have eyes that see us
even if our names no longer signify,

even if we hurry into shelters out of range
of all pernicious influence.
We matter to ourselves as workers matter

to their factories, useless
in the darkened theater of the third-growth trees,
as if the world had shrugged

and turned away, having said
the perfect thing.

With My Senses in Ruins

Here's a recipe for seeing: slow green sleep,
and feeling as a long-expected season feels
the day the sky entrusts its new campaign

of sails and sheets. Where in time do figures,
half-imagined, blend themselves with lawns
as standards blend with all exceptions?

Always the same, or same-ish, bank of low
suggestive clouds, the freshness of the air
in theory. Charcoal smudges under trees

across a reach of dried-up swamp relate
to passions forcefully declared then left

to fade, like fragrances. What's wanted: light,
in which the ends throw shadows and the means
retreat, uncovering a floodplain where

memorials, deployed at intervals,
describe a pattern unaccounted for
among the new curations. Where in time

does darkness, not sustainable, give way
to brightnesses the ur-ironic must abjure?
In the rough impasto of the leaves

a gunship hoists its signal. The rundown trees
throw lattices across the stream.

1971

Each night the station signoff's cherry blossoms plunge
before a flag, and deck guns demonstrate their mouths.
The network's eagle banks into electric snow,
midnight's white brain, before the anthem augurs how
to raise white crosses over killed boys' graves in twelves.
The camera tilts and wheels above the Capitol,
its empty plazas and its effigies of dead
white men, then pans across the river bearing coins
and bright medallions on its surface to the sea.
The bugle's voice conceives two dozen notes to set
the white sun in its static shroud. Awake all night.
A hot white wind patrols the Massachusetts towns.

How It Ends

It rained and it rained and it rained
and in the end
people just left their stuff
and went off somewhere to die
like tired old dogs

In the vaguelight promise of the drowned city
two Italian shopkeepers
argued bitterly over something
that couldn't possibly still matter
and in the end
they threw their heavy aluminum café chairs into the water
although the shoreline had mostly
been erased by then
and it was just waves rolling in between the sidewalks
and up the marble steps of banks

Some rich guy figured out
how to stoke a machine
with various sized vials of gold powder
to simulate his daily presence with a show
of pressures and differences
but it didn't give much satisfaction and anyway
for what audience beyond
his own estranged imagination

I didn't want to die but in the end
the city made a pano of rainflood
and cars idled on the streetsides
with the toopink light of the cobraheads
glaring in their eyes
and burnishing their curves
in the latest styles

I didn't know how to get out of this life
but then again
that's always been the problem
hasn't it

THE HORSEMEN OF THE ICE

Some could not believe it was happening, even as the oceans rose
like sucked-in breath, even as the current died in the wires
blinding the eyes of the useless TVs,

                       even as the houses on the shoreline
dropped into the harbor one by one,

                       like fruit from overhanging trees.

It was a new chance for the crows,

                   blank and clicking in their murders,
                   picking out the eyes of the downtown corpses,

such that none would dare walk past them on the way
from warehouse store to hideout.

                  No one ate the windfall apples
                  for the noise they made.

––––––––––––

Sunlight fell in the empty streets,
on roses rioting in arbors.

––––––––––––

The people cared for the world

                 but had forgotten how to tell it.

So many furtive in the streets with their breakage,
steering with their gaspump hands,

                    staring with their flatscreen eyes,
                    and with their mousewheel fingers
pointing and clicking.

———————————

Then the machines that ate the topsoil stalled.

Jimson weed and sawgrass swallowed up
the fields.

                    The farmhouse's brows collapsed
and the creeks once choked with slag ran free.

———————————

The farmer and his wife slept in their bed,
the farmer's many children slept in their beds, the farmhands
slept in their beds, and the fields threw over them
a cold green sheet,

                stopped up their mouths and eyes,

and they slept.

———————————

The empire of the seed-corn fell, and sawgrass broke
the backs of the roads.

————————

My brain felt good inside my head
as the sun expired and the horsemen of the ice
                                        rode out.

I found their confusion beautiful:
the deathlovers and the lifehaters driven
                            through the same red fuse.

HER FAVORITE BOOK

smelled of Red Astrachan apples and rust

smelled of library   the long untethered afternoons

made like any book a door

She gripped it as its red
skin puckered from its spine
she cradled it   the gold
                              stamping on its boards defaced
                              by her attentions

————————

Big light blistered through the cunning trees   magnolia
white ash   Carolina silverbell with sawtoothed leaves   Sharp
electric smells of severed grasses mixed

          with smells of watered dust and dusted rain
          Little balled-up fists of rain
          hanging in the highest leaves   *Hush-a-bye babes, don't you cry*

          she sing-songed to herself   a practice mother
          trying on a kindness

          like a Sunday dress

————————

She read   in August heat   and felt the stitching of her shorts-hem
bite into her thigh   She tasted metal

in the socket where her last front tooth
had fallen out

        imagining herself a hundred years ago
        and ten years older   capable   mature

        as she and Clara Barton
        bound up men's strange wounds with husks

        there being no more bandages

———————————

The book smelled of care and chloroform and suffering
of pain and battle and the cries

of wounded soldiers bleeding in Antietam mud
or freezing in the drifts at Fredericksburg

                swarms of black flakes
                falling in their faces

———————————

Shoeless gloveless ragged   wringing blood out
of her laden skirt, she waded to the far
red bank of Acquia Creek with loads of biscuits
and supplies

Virginia, bring that saw and lantern here   She bent above
the vague white faces, speaking to her

now and then of mothers daughters sweethearts wives

It pleased her to be tending men despite the grimness
and the strain   to earn their gratitude and curb their pain

—————————

Her father, dead already seven years—
beyond her help   beyond her memory

She bent above him in her favorite book and sheared
.his ruined limb away   *Hush my baby, don't you cry*

—each stroke of the saw blade

binding her to him

letting her inside him

cutting her to bone

Exodus

We crossed to Egypt's

> desert edge: blasted egg-
> shell, ecru-and-camel
> camouflage,

> dunes like racks of wedding cakes the Red
> Sea ate a shore into.

> And left its rim of salt against, devouring the sweetness.

We went beyond our fear, our bare or sandaled feet
    working in the drifts,

> while Pharaoh's cavalry, all silk,
> chalcedony, and iron, arced the gap.

Behind them, Pithom vanished into sand.

Before us rose the wayless Sea.

The elder struck the bronze-cuffed butt-end of his staff three times
against a blistered stone, which drove the waters up

                  in two high cataracts of blood,
arrowed by a path of mud.

Angelfish and moray eel gasped and foundered on the track, we crushed them
with our heels, we raced between
                              two lifted blood-cliffs
at dream-speed, deafened.

Then we found ourselves across. Amenhotep's horsemen closed behind us,
stallions stumbling in the slime and fish-slick, boot-soles
                                            slipping in the stirrups.

The elder split his staff against a stone. The curdled waters rushed
to meet above the tumbled heads

of men and horses screaming as the breech collapsed
and stove them in,
                  horse-foam feeding sea-foam in the redder
sea—then silence as the littered corpses lurched ashore.
                                        We turned
and saw the wilderness of Shur:
                        blasted egg-
                        shell, ecru-and-camel
                        camouflage,

                        bitter waters both
                        before us and behind us

while our songs in praise of death went up to God.

THE CONDITION OF MATTER
Hurricane Katrina

Listen! There were corpses all over the city.

Everywhere the couple walked they startled
cavalries of flies. Gold, blood, and turquoise

friendship beads twisted in the limbs
of torn up liveoak slammed through walls,
tangled up with lines

across which charges sparked and fizzed.

The couple walked three days in rags,
ignored by Guards and volunteers, their few
belongings stashed in plastic bags—

They thought of Pearl River, where her father lived,
—no news about his parish on the one
surviving station. She was too afraid

to fear, or too exhausted for her fear
to frighten her. Something in her
broke, the way the storm surge burst

the levee at the 17th Street canal:
Too much desire.

———————————

Three days past the eyewall and the eye,
she'd eaten nothing but a Zero bar a boy
sprinting from a gas station's gashed side

gave her from his pilfered stash.

She started to imagine riders
gliding in the wreckage, black and helmeted
as in a B-movie apocalypse,

gliding in to sweep the city

of its sprung debris. They drifted
down Calliope and Clio and the Ponchartrain
Expressway toward a checkpoint

—She followed one, she saw the cold

cloud of his exhalations massing up
above the glare of shit and spent perfumes.
It was mercy for the god to hide his face,

the rider breathed. *Mercy for the storm*

to sheath the knife-blade
of his face. Mercy the catastrophe.
Mercy that the waters rise.

The couple came with hundreds of their outcast kin,

like Israelites approaching Aqaba,
to cross to Gretna on the dry West Bank,
but a line of sheriffs barred the foot

of the Crescent City Connection, firing

over their heads to drive them back
down the steep incline of the bridge
into the city that had flushed them out.

The condition of matter is exile, that it might return.

Her husband shouted to her where she stood
among the husks of shelters blown to bits
by rotor-wash, her face gone incandescent

in the metal wind—among the husks she took

the moment in undimmed, although it burned her guts.
She took it in and took it in, until her husband
seized her, shoved her through the chopper doors,

which killed the circuit, and they lifted off.

THE WALL OF JERUSALEM ALSO IS BROKEN DOWN, AND THE GATES THEREOF ARE BURNED WITH FIRE
Nehemiah 1:3

I held your hand the last time. You looked so lovely
in your trashbag jacket. Your unfed arms showed white
and slender poking out, like lengths of pipe, your hair
a mass of swept-back wires. We paused a moment
on the cliff where half our neighborhood fell in.

Because our rage had dropped away, and all ambition,
we were free to wander, if we wanted to, down
the dried-up streambeds, or clamber up
among the metal cities of the power grid—
dead coils and spires, from which the living charge had fled.

The evening came on so serene, with flocks
of black unhurried birds alighting where they would,
discoloring the shrouds. That man who slumped
against the storefront glass—I won't forget him—
slept. You let him. Anyway, he couldn't use our help.

You'd lost your last few labor pounds, and you were proud,
and so was I, of how your skin stretched taut
along your jawline, and the model profile
of your hips. We pushed the empty carriage
in a cellar hole. At last, you had the look.

I held your hand. Your fingers, slim and dry
as shielded wire, trembled with the current
passing through them, trembled as the flameteeth bit
along the rooftops, trembled as the beams shrugged in
and as the maples—green, then smoke, then red—

went up along the landfill's edge, relinquishing
their warehoused calories. Fire sang
along the useless streets, spat in gardens,
sighed where steeples showed their ribs and ceased.
What a silence we maintained, while blazes hissed

and licked and bled, how patient, gentle, and solicitous,
without support from preachers, books, or therapists!
We listened as the rain came dropping
through the burnt-out trees. The fire loved us, made us safe,
accepted every bit of us, til we were all devoured.

COLLAGE

Passing along a familiar street
I carry seeds in a dried-up pod,
baby's rattle or future's proof or both.

Sunglasses, smartphone, coffee:
generations of waste both blond and black.
Even colors have constituencies.

Light, that is to say
poison. Death, that is to say
recycling. All these people with their hair

and clothings, cars the color of nothing
found in nature, ripped
paper sounds of engines, roadside burnings,

edges of dark gray spills. Drawn with them
through the glass funnel of a Starbucks
soon to be disgorged. Over clouds

pass lighter clouds or is it smoke,
seriously? Morning faces too slippery to catch
and I can't pull the right-hand door

to hear the strip mall sparrows'
knotted song, woman in a thin chemise
outside, moaning smoke.

PROGRESS TOWARD DISAPPEARANCE

I raft against slack water, waiting. Where
my bow slipped now two wavelets deliquesce.
Smooth surface: how to live like that, unhurried

at the banks, not caring how the reed stems
bend their heads, nor how the water skaters
punctuate the river's sheen. I feel this full

impermanence: green rocks, green drift, green fish,
a fall of whitened flowers from a branch.
I have no time to swallow time, which means

I'm swallowed. Thrushes blare their old same song,
while shadows under pines pretend a refuge.

———————————

Last year's oak leaves clatter at the limbs' ends. Fair winds
scatter on the surface of the water names no eye
is fast enough to read. And since there's nothing now unstained,

I place this shouting copter in its sky. No matter:
Past the dams, where reedbanks brake the wind,
the arguments of many geese advance. A miracle

they winter here, beneath these diesel fumes and propjet shrieks.
Dear geese, I too adore this houseless reach, that scrim
of dark denuded trees, these scraps and stumps and weeds

I drive obliviously by most afternoons,
enclosed inside surmountable removes.

NECROPASTORALS

[1]
Disruption of the warblers' routes   Parched white hair
of brome and grama

Conifers retreating upslope   Dominion
of the dry white oak

The woods propose a blind white room   then burn

[2]
A white   accessible

              only through green   A black
              contracted

                    as a plague

                    of fern fronds chokes
                    this gully

Not yet bone
No longer crisp

Root threads inching down the colorspace

from succulent
to dread

[3]
When no human person's here
the pine woods brim with sound
rare in the galaxy

It matters

Crabgrass silts a drainage ditch
with pointless green
My word for sacred is undisturbed

[4]
Beneath the earth's skin lies
          a face   Black oak knuckles

clench it   Citizens have sieved
               down through it

to the soil
Dead seeds swollen black   laxing

where the blind-eyed beetles
harvest rot for keep

[5]
The white pine's

awl might strike and wake
the blinded face

Long sentences of cadmium and acids
scribbled on the wetlands

a profanity vital in the otter's mouth
who sine-waves over ice fields with his death

already messaged in his spine

Wedged between his ribs a gift

(the gift a flaw the flaw a wound)
from which his blood's black liquor flows

A second body running out
across the smoking snow

[6]
Look inside the box to think outside the box

Boxes made for holding goods or corpses
Corpsewood boxes made from clearcuts

Nothing's clear in a denuded landscape
but nobody's looking as shadows clock over footpaths

on a football afternoon with the light
going out of the sky
earlier and earlier

and the bluescreened faces
of the fiercest predators the earth has ever seen
pretend to a devastating mildness

There's such a thing in the world now
as "nature deficit disorder"
which means it may be too late

as names make boxes to hold the memories of things
that have almost finished vanishing

[7]
If my need were less dire I'd be assailed
by less silence
                    here among the beardtongue
and strawberry clover   Otters cottontails hawks jays loves

why have you savaged your faces
against me
                    (Rapacious Pilgrims ghosting
over grass   I hear you passing
and the skins of the dead you wore)
                                    If I were less human
you could be more so   I made a botch
but didn't blare it   which ought

to count
              and who am I now   What waste
have I assembled and is it part of me
this rat's long tail

[8]
The asshole trees shit seeds
which fuck the darkness underground

sucking till the wet threads come

death in its other aspect
the series' prequel

waste light vomited in pools

to stink and bleed
into delicate fringes

[9]
When the woods stand empty there will be no woods
and incarnation's tensioned wire
will warp and straighten and its pain
will never end

My Own Most Familiar Sensation

To have lived long enough, and to have seen
far enough, is to have become
a connoisseur of disappearances.

My favorite time of day is that transition
when the last light lessens from the sky,
leaving an impression of rooflines and willow limbs

where just a moment earlier they stood forth
with such ferocious clarity that I
completely failed to apprehend them. Is the law

that recognition trembles at the seam
where seeing meets extinction? So the line

continues to its edge, then plunges
into absence. So the fox that glimmers through the cone
my headlights swing across the yard.

And so my memory, a vapor trail,
dissolves as I approach, the other way,
that stop past which my total shape

will tremble into view, a photograph
that I, by definition, cannot ever see.
Nor can I see those prior me's, those gone

Jonathans, except as constructs, pictures
that I conjure up from colored bits

and lines that by themselves show nothing
but the path from non-existence to erasure:
shadows with an intervening gap.

Last night I walked a line from home
without a definite trajectory and watched
the wind come pouring over Carver Hill,

creaking and thrashing the birch limbs
while lights winked on and off beyond the branches.
Who watched before such things as lights,

and who will watch hereafter? At each extreme,
the answer's "no one." I can almost see it.

AN ALGAE MAT ON THE WATER

I lie awake at night, alone, the bedsheets
moonlight-striped or shadowed by the new
moon's dark. The gods who regulate our lives

are blind to us, as we are blind to them.
They go by many names—Division, Membrane,
Slippage, Edge—but never answer when

we call. I wonder if they're really there, as I
attend the pre-dawn silence. Is it nothing,
or the echo of an axiom

that bears no argument? A proposition
one assumes: we're subject, fugitive,

impermanent as shine, as algae snagged
against a logjam which a cow moose care-
lessly dislodges with her left hind hoof.

Her thoughtlessness announces an ideal;
the algae's frailty confirms a certainty.
I wait. Eventually those clouds will clear

the pines that edge the yard. A light will strike
down from the sky, and then the dark will strike.
Such terrors we conceive, and then we make them.

So much for good.
So much for the imagination.

Darkness, brightness, further dark: such structure,
simple though it seems, exceeds us. Why
not simply gaze, refract, record? The eye

as pinhole aperture; the mind as dark
receptive camera which accepts the light.
Can disbelief become a creed? For I

believe in wind deforming water, bent
and unbent grass, whatever stands forth brightly
from the flux. In its dominion over

nothing, substance only proves divine.
Out of absence flares a temporary shine.

In Human Form but Ghostly

A train of shadows maneuvers eastward,
entering the dark arch where a river,
dry almost down to its stones, still flows out,

writing a silver line across the valley,
a line whose argument is perspective,
convergence, dispersal, the absence

at the heart of every apprehension.
In the hollow at the back of my head,
for instance, stood a range of mountains, high

in childhood, now a line of worn-down hills
subtracting color from the radiation.

My dissipated enthusiasms
have the power to blow the planets backwards
in their orbits, or feel as though they do.

As the communications frequencies
fill with chatter and a darkness grows that
no human language can dispel, I slip

into a vanishing interval crammed
with sound. Poised here in a green lacuna
between construction sites, I haunt the sheer

unlikelihood of all this shine, these snagged
perspectives, these disappearing lines.

Forest Panel

We are going to live on in dry amazement,
          aren't we? Yes. But where will all the graveyards go
with their thwarted hands? We tidy up the firmament,
          now indigo,

although it didn't need it. Laid-off bees,
          sullen and pugnacious in a honeysuckle shade,
turn, like darling enemies,
          to signal smoke, to night. The motorcade

of summer stars comes roaring over and
          we cannot hear to hear. Can we? No.
Our ears are full of ampersands.
          For hours we haunt the old casino

by the stream, chip-
          strewn, dice of broken oaks, roulettes
of robins' nests. Canaries *sip, sip, sip*
          their courtesy drinks. Is there any region yet

unbranded? We are going to live on
          despite
incursions in the genome. Right?
          What emergent hand or eye? What unexpected patterns in the light?

Poem Beginning with the Line at the Edge of a Mass of Dark Cloud, Which Takes the Yellow Light

It isn't nothing, but it will be. How
        the gold succumbs, the starving lavender.
A city, slammed up on another city, builds
        toward dirtied whitenesses. This *is*

the long witness, taking every shape, eternal, and the bright day
        will not end. I'm afraid I've purchased safety
with entitlement and blood. The moon's a white
        half of a half-dollar,

and when the church bells chime I use the whole chime-box,
        I use every chime. The privilege
of two yellow houses standing close
        by the harbor, the in-curling tide

that drowns a folding chair, a dock with its feet
        in the water, a dory orange
on the reach, a lighter stacked with ruined boxes,
        flags in the wind like hatless heads,

dark clouds folding and unfolding, sky:
        the delicious feel of the syllable, the lip
licked and made explicit. How brilliant, to be merged with the blue.
        Estrangement is only human.

Sea Panel

Someone is wading into a desert of abandoned light
                without a hat or a bottle of water
or even shoes. Look how the light swirls around her calves,
                making little white swirl-lines

as in a painting by Hokusai. She's wearing a white
                or very pale blue thigh-length dress, someone's daughter
or wife, and a spill of dark hair down her back. She laughs,
                or something makes her shudder. The lines

of her dress straps, the ladder of her hair, her height:
                the only verticals. It's getting hotter,
she's wading deeper, nobody can stop her. In half
                an hour, she'll be gone. The surface shines.

Wait. Come back. Along the horizon, the bright
                face of a cargo ship goes dazzling, a freighter
turning sideways to the sun beneath a farrago of rough
                red clouds. In antique times,

the small dark comma of a boat
                would ride the sea's long sentence. Later,
there were maps with great abandoned stretches:
                "Here there be monsters. Death for those who enter."

Torn Panel

Others were just throwing a veil over suffering,
               but it was too late, I could still see the
blue toes sticking out, the big toe and the next two toes
               on the naked foot, and in fact,

because the light bled through the veil a little,
               I could see its hunched-up body,
surprisingly small, like a frightened girl's
               or a rumor before it spreads,

and over the veil a pattern of grapevines
               reached its rivulets of veins, with spade-shaped leaves
and sparrows. A meager snow began,
               and then a thicker snow, which laid a blanket

on the veil. You would have thought the girl, if it was a girl,
               had simply gone to sleep there, on the trail beside
the hardened arteries of tree trunks and
               the branches intricate as sectioned brains.

Such a small and unassuming thing, so reticent
               and tender that I fell in love with her
the way one falls in love with one's own
               contingent spit-and tissue-paper self.

Look: there's sleep, and when the body disunites
            the moon spills upward in the sky,
the last white pill from the bottle, and throws
            its analgesic brilliance over all the world.

INCARNATION PANEL

A small peculiarity of mesh and carbon rose from nothing,
                designed by no one, but with a pattern
everyone could recognize. Such is the record
                written on the body: the cells' emergent calculus, then

a plunge described by ones and zeroes toward a mill
                through which the waters of a poisoned river
fall, engaging its great red wheel. I remember how the lifeboats
                drifted from the wreckage

with their cargoes of stars and particles. Holes had been torn
                in the net of pure space, and inside I could see my father's hands
before the honey had unstrung them.
                The ones made accidents, the zeroes followed,

until the sky's blue surface looked for all the world like a calm
                that one could plummet through. Dumb in the forest
I came to myself, and though I was almost blind, I pledged allegiance
                to the flag of the united states of the visible.

GOLD PANEL
distantly seen

Close at hand I keep, unswerved by
                anthropomorphizing gestures in the trees, their
matter camouflage of meanings more than
                tacky imagery of green. By shadow swerved.

And at horizon gold-flaked, scarce-precious,
                availing maws and cones that, having been,
now alter spaciousness. Close at hand I keep,
                a straw of bendy light as into my field

holes and orchards rise and fly, a serial told
                in crow japes, cricket quavers, low strokes of the soon
to be silenced. Cold close, this cloud of houses,
                boson-born and –headed. Water. Figures

in my kept rooms, an occasion of clouds,
                lucite blossoms blown to ash, not seed. And
where is my love, for all that? *In* it, *in*
                the fluxion, mad for change within a scaffold

constitutionally permanent. Articulations *in*
                the damage. So my close misfires, the forced
adjacencies. Between the houses and the crows. Between the
                body and the not I bathe in and can never know.

GARDEN PANEL

I will accept the citizenship of my exile
           only when September's tenure
clasps this ruined landscape with a kind
           of sumptuous regret. *Sumptuous*:

to be in love with oceans among orchards.
           As if an apple were the sign
of unfulfillable desire, reflecting only what it can't absorb,
           like color. Fallen apples, spotted apples,

apples wormed and sweet,
           up to their tropics of cancer with runoff.
Isn't this the very lesson of the fall—
           what happens when you take your satisfactions

only from the fruits you don't desire?
           Above me, dark flocks pass
before they register, black flecks blown across their feathers.
           As if the swamp beyond the orchard

were a factory, as if regret
           had made still pools thrumming with hatchlings
under ash and buckthorn, bright rot
           spreading under snags.

I will accept the citizenship of my exile
           only to repair the godshaped hole blown into the roof of the world
through which innumerable particles pour
           like waste, or persons.

∞∞∞

THE MANNEQUIN POET LAUREATE ADDRESSES HER AUDIENCE

after Isa Genzken

Persons of plastic   posed or poised
Long live the vinyl body   the jointed
composite body   and the fall

                    of nylon hair
                    pink or fire-warden orange
                    always perfect   never subject or infringed

                    once fitted there

I sing the body inorganic and

the body's ruin   how the frame   impinged
by threat or fashion   falls   between the genders

              Wounded from the inside out
                    a red acrylic spreads   beneath protections
              and you're braver than the dying ones   you're more
                  interior

Faced   or faceless
                    sex   and terror
          shelter   and emergency
                              and your godlike apostasy

I don't believe in arguments from design
There is just this world of constant lights and traffics as

          the silence of the lifeless future bleeds
                    its oils backwards into the fabric

                    and the canvas has no edge but spills
          its ruin over all the world
                              Here

creep   wretch   inside this barrel

                              Wrap your face with wool
                                        or steel   Kill
                    with thinness as a blade
                              might kill

Make frailty your faith
and over all
be still   now and forever
technical   louche

            enlisted   Teach your children
                to burlesque the thermoplastic plenum
            represented here by golf balls
                lifted in a classical hand

a gesture troubled with significance   rising

if it rises   to the streetlights' height

            the city's event horizon

            beyond which nothing can be seen

            because of the nothing that is there

SHIPWRECKS

Wind in the half-oak high
    as two stacked houses
catches with the sound
    of flames on dry
pitched paper. Thousands,
    maybe, have drowned

with that havoc in their ears,
    just offshore, their tears
mingling with that other salt.
    It's no one's fault:
ships will snap their sheets,
    and sailors' feet

will founder with the undertow.
    Now the sky-rasp
ratchets hard, the wind-grasp
    turns the leaves' pale-as-snow
undersides over, meaning rain.
    But the evening air retains

something of its heat,
    and a tawny light
emerges from a late cloud.
    On shore, a growing crowd
watched the sailors fight
    against their sure defeat.

We watch each other go
    down hard, and though
we send up texts and flares
    we often can't get through.
The oak will shake its dried-up hair.
    There's nothing we can do.

Me and the Fly

I would like to write about this fly
with whom I'm sharing this house for a while

To him this house is eternal
or nearly so

It has stood here in the town of Harvard
for two thousand nine hundred and ninety of its generations

which in human time
would equal one hundred and seventy-six thousand seven hundred and seventy-seven years

as though the house had been built all wood-framed and Federal
in the Rancholabrean faunal age of the Middle Pleistocene

when Neanderthals were stacking stalagmites four deep in caves in France
and mammoths stomped the ice sheets three thousand feet thick above Carbondale

But I who have the slower eyes
can almost see the house decaying

I can see that the mantle
above the living room fireplace needs replacing

because of settling
and maybe rot in the walls

and the floors have warped like slow rollers
breaking against the baseboards

that were painted this past summer
which was in the childhood of the fly's great-great-grandparents

I feel the impulse to crush this fly
with a rolled up copy of *The New Yorker*

or to whack it like a tennis ball
with Robert Lowell's *Collected Poems*

but I relent
and open the bathroom window sash enough for the fly to escape

to whatever remains of his life
and I to the blink of mine

Why not think of the time elapsed since the last magnetic pole reversal
seven hundred and eighty thousand years ago

The continents ride on cells of boiling magma
like blocks of styrofoam on a lake

and the cells in the backs of my hands
grow weary of making their shape

and they lag and buckle
like a suspect terrain

At the Bottom of the Sea in Montana

I'm coming up
from Billings to the Bighorn

burning cheap Dakota gas

in a rented Dodge the color of a face
forgotten in a bad dream,

the face of a former version of myself

sprawled across a motel bed, or the color
of the wall just beyond the face,

a sort of putty, the color that nothingness

might choose to be painted, if nothingness
were a motel room you could disappear in.

Along I-90, in the windy early morning glare

of south central Montana,
three ranch hands lean against a fence line,

looming up and swiftly

falling away
like any common road sign—

Hardin, Crow Agency, Garryowen,

towns in the blank of the map, as though
nothing with a name could live there.

Which isn't so, I know, and yet they float

like plankton, weightless in a sea of light.
The first guy gloves the rail, proprietary;

the next one's baseball cap's a tatter

of a dirty flag; the last guy spits
and twists, his t-shirt damp

and grimed the color of a recent grave.

———————————

In a valley close to here,
shadows cast by nameless ridgelines

run their tongues

over Little Bighorn headstones.
Warm and eager tongues, like dogs',

they lick without discrimination,

wetting everything until it all becomes
the same dull color.

Custer didn't lose:

each year he's resurrected,
ringlets daubed with cinnamon

and skewered newly on a Cheyenne lance,

in case you didn't get the message.
Sunlight glances off gilt epaulettes.

It's all white money now.

The silence after reenactment
stirs its fingers in the grass,

redeeming nothing.

And if the children killed at random
sleep in no marked graves, remember:

night will flood these valleys like a sea

full of strange suspended shadows,
its weight increasing

year by year,

and crush all traces of us out,
the sea floor putty-blank,

nothing walking there,

and on the surface angels,
if the testament can be believed,

wrapping caution tape around the earth.

———————————

At a rest stop north of Lodge Grass,
before the land tilts uphill toward Wyoming

and the pines begin assembling on its slopes

to make the landscape seem
more normal,

I pull over in the early glitter,

drawn by something I'm afraid to name.
Wind comes fluming down the basin

of the dry Cretaceous Seaway

driving parodies of waves
before it through the white hard grass.

Is anything benign?

I've locked a silence in the trunk
as final as a former self,

my right hand rigorous

around a basement key
I thought I'd long discarded.

So many unmined strata,

creatures mute but perfect,
frozen as they fell.

The silence grows beyond all bearing now;

even the wind scouring down the valley,
commonplace and fatal,

can no longer dispel it,

its sound
a version of the silence,

something *in* the silence, obstreperous

but meaningless,
like radio signals from a nebula.

All those leagues of air above,

and then an endless darkness,
and us abandoned at the bottom,

hoping to be heard.

—————————————

Because the wind comes hailing down this freeway
like the ghost of history,

and will not stop until the body

longs to burst, releasing
what is trapped inside

to add its bitty eddy to the surge,

the ranch hand steers his half-ton
down to Hardin, where he has a date

to pick up Betsy, double-shifting

at the Silver Fox. *Another decent haul,*
she tells him, brandishing a wad.

I made good bank.

They drive some distance up a two-track
in the hills. Everything they move through

has been paid in blood

the government demanded
as a tax on absence.

Its redness dozes in the clay

the faithless rain makes umber putty of,
and in the grass

the moon's ironic rising copper

can't entirely blanch,
and in the magpie's louche, facetious eye,

though likely closed in sleep

or such oblivion as the magpie can command.
The valley spreads below,

a flat, dark harbor.

Once, a sea a half-mile deep
lolled through here,

splitting North American in two.

The bones of those who swam there
settle stoned and deep:

plesiosaurs and ammonites, gigantic sharks

and mosasaurs the length of 18-wheelers.
The sky went black

with pterosaurs, as numerous

as pigeons. Gone, for eighty million years.
And pointless,

all that birth and radiating blood,

and nothing at the end
but heat and dust?

Nothing but a blank machine,

unless it leads to us?
Betsy leans against her man

and sighs, her face a shade

of putty in the moonlight.
She doesn't think, *In eighty million years* . . .

The whorl inside her,

the latticeworks and acids, the current
hastening from her to him,

wave-form, particle, breath and frame:

it's there,
and then it isn't there,

and then the wind blows every trace of it away.

HISTORY

Fearsome in his superhero sneakers, Jonah rides.
The light in the right shoe isn't working; the left one
signals when he pedals. Down the sidewalk, crazy
with an after-dinner joy, he shouts and twitches on his seat,
snapping his helmet-hidden head one way and then another,
shadowed-on by early leaves and clouds he won't remember:

Perfect. Up the driveway, with the wind disordering
the neighbor's tall white pines, he parks his bike and goes inside,
the dancer-conqueror, and downs a slice of watermelon, red part
and a bit of crisp white rind. Later, during pre-bed rituals,
I hold his small electric body in my iffy hands,
coaxing on his socks and two-piece PJs.

At length his light winks out, and then the others, and the distance
in the darkened earth grows farther. Sometimes only dreams
can reach us where we lie. Opened in the silenced house
like books, our bodies fill with brilliant likenesses: the father dead
almost a year, the dark-haired friend who in this version
doesn't turn on you, the sad-eyed emissary from the mountain.

On the porch, the landlord's vine grows bitter on its lattice,
and the poison stars, exploding in their traces, cluster in the west.
Is there any fended ground in all the earth? When Genghis Khan

invaded Helmand, helmet-headed riders sowed the fields with salt.
They've found archaic scallop shells on peaks in Appalachia.
Foxes quit the bulldozed acres built with model houses.

Patient in the night wind, the white pines wait for us
to not be here again.

NOTES

"Tilted City," "Lined Up Just So," "Progress Toward Disappearance," "With My Senses in Ruins," "An Algae Mat on the Water," "My Own Most Familiar Sensation," and "In Human Form but Ghostly" take their titles from poems in the second half of *As Much As, If Not More Than* by H. L. Hix (Etruscan Press, 2014).

"The Horsemen of the Ice" is for Kevin Prufer.

"Her Favorite Book" is for Maureen Wittbold. It borrows some phrases and images from Cathy East Dubowski's young adult biography *Clara Barton: Healing the Wounds* (Silver Burdett Press, 1991).

Many of the details in "The Condition of Matter" come from survivor blogs and foreign newspaper accounts of the aftermath of Hurricane Katrina in New Orleans.

"In Human Form but Ghostly" responds indirectly to the poem "By the Allegheny" in *The Moon Before Morning* by W. S. Merwin (Copper Canyon Press, 2015).

The first line of "Forest Panel" is from Brenda Hillman's poem "Franciscan Complex," published in *Cascadia* (Wesleyan University Press, 2001).

The first line of "Torn Panel" is from Dana Levin's poem "Quelquechose," published in *Wedding Day* (Copper Canyon Press, 2005).

The first line of "Sea Panel" is from Karla Kelsey's poem "Of Contiguity and Fracture," published in *Boston Review*, Feb/Mar2004, Vol. 29 Issue 1, p. 52.

The first line of "Garden Panel" is from G. C. Waldrep's poem "[after the murder]," published in *Goldbeater's Skin* (Center for Literary Publishing at Colorado State University, 2003).

Acknowledgments

I am grateful to the editors of the journals in which the following poems first appeared, sometimes in different versions:

The Cincinnati Review: "Sea Panel," "Garden Panel"
Copper Nickel: "Tilted City," "The Story of My Life"
The Cresset: "Lined Up Just So," "An Algae Mat on the Water"
Green Mountains Review: "The Condition of Matter"
Harvard Review: "History"
Kenyon Review: "Her Favorite Book"
Mānoa: A Pacific Journal of International Writing: "Necropastorals"
Notre Dame Review: "Exodus" (as "Report of the Witness / III")
Pleiades: "The Wall of Jerusalem Also Is Broken Down, and the Gates Thereof
     Are Burned with Fire"
Plume: "With My Senses in Ruins"
Southwest Review: "Forest Panel"
Unsplendid: "Shipwrecks"
Witness: "The Horsemen of the Ice" (as "Report of the Witness")

"Tilted City" won the *Copper Nickel* Editors' Prize in Poetry for Issue 21, Fall 2015
"History" appeared on *Poetry Daily* (poems.com) on November 27, 2013.
"Her Favorite Book" was republished online at *Redux* (www.reduxlitjournal.com).

This book was a long time in the making, so I have a number of friends and fellow writers to thank for their encouragement and commentary. My gratitude, then, to Amy M. Clark and the other members of our long-ago writing group:

Brian Burt, Jennifer Flescher, Cecily Parks, Mike Perrow, Lynne Potts, and Leslie Williams. To Martha Collins, Molly Peacock, and Kevin Prufer for their insightful readings of the project as a whole. To Carolyn Forché, Victoria Redel, and Alan Shapiro for their superlative workshops at the Fine Arts Work Center in Provincetown, Massachusetts, where some of these poems first struggled into the light. To Joan Houlihan for the friendship and the endless cups of coffee, and for organizing the Colrain Poetry Manuscript Conferences. To Rane Arroyo, Kristina Bicher, Rebecca Foust, Marci Rae Johnson, Maxima Kahn, and Elizabeth Majerus for their readings of individual poems. To Mark Irwin for the collaborations. To Wayne Miller for all the support. To the Ucross Foundation for the time and space to write, and to the Massachusetts Cultural Council for the generous grant. To Henry Israeli, Christopher Salerno, and the rest of the staff at Saturnalia Books for believing in this book and for bringing it out into the world. And to Harvey Hix, for the inspiration and the ongoing exchanges, over the many years and the many miles.

Also by Jonathan Weinert:

In the Mode of Disappearance

Thirteen Small Apostrophes

*Until Everything Is Continuous Again: American Poets
on the Recent Work of W. S. Merwin*

A Slow Green Sleep is printed in Adobe CaslonPro.
www.saturnaliabooks.org